Labor Day

by Meredith Dash

ABDO

NATIONAL HOLIDAYS

Kids

www.abdopublishing.com

Published by Abdo Kids, a division of ABDO, PO Box 398166, Minneapolis, Minnesota 55439.

Copyright © 2015 by Abdo Consulting Group, Inc. International copyrights reserved in all countries. No part of this book may be reproduced in any form without written permission from the publisher.

Printed in the United States of America, North Mankato, Minnesota.

052014

092014

Photo Credits: Alamy, Getty Images, Old Oregon Photos, Shutterstock, Thinkstock, © Kelly Short, Lewis W. Hine / CC-BY-SA-2.0 p.7, © Iakov Filimonov / Shutterstock.com p.21

Production Contributors: Teddy Borth, Jennie Forsberg, Grace Hansen

Design Contributors: Candice Keimig, Laura Rask, Dorothy Toth

Library of Congress Control Number: 2013952080

Cataloging-in-Publication Data

Dash, Meredith.

Labor Day / Meredith Dash.

p. cm. -- (National holidays)

ISBN 978-1-62970-044-1 (lib. bdg.)

Includes bibliographical references and index.

1. Labor Day--Juvenile literature.   I. Title.

394.264--dc23

2013952080

Table of Contents

Labor Day

Labor Day **honors** American
workers. Workers make our
nation strong.

4

History

People worked very

long days in the 1800s.

Even children worked.

It was a hard life.

6

7

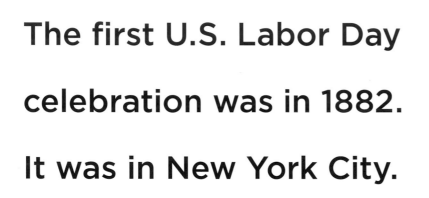

The first U.S. Labor Day

celebration was in 1882.

It was in New York City.

Labor Day was meant
to give workers a voice.
Workers joined together.
They wanted better working
conditions. They wanted rights.

11

New York City celebrated year after year. Workers marched in parades. Working **conditions** were getting better.

13

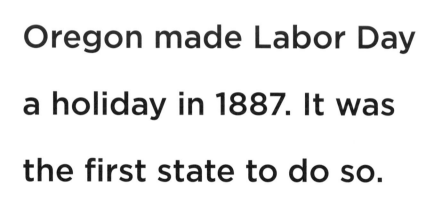

Oregon made Labor Day a holiday in 1887. It was the first state to do so.

15

On June 28, 1894, Labor Day became a **national holiday**. President Grover Cleveland signed it into law.

17

Today's Labor Day

We celebrate Labor Day on the first Monday in September. Workers **enjoy** a day off from work.

Many countries observe a similar holiday. It is sometimes called Workers' Day. It occurs on May 1st.

More Facts

- A long time ago, workers were paid very little and worked very long days. Even small children worked.

- Originally, Labor Day was used as a day to discuss plans for better working **conditions**.

- Today, Labor Day is a day for workers to relax and feel appreciated!

22

Glossary

condition – the way something is.

enjoy – to find happiness in.

honor – to pay respect to.

national holiday – a special event celebrated by a country.

Index

abdokids.com

Use this code to log on to abdokids.com and access crafts, games, videos and more!

Abdo Kids Code:
NLK0441